D1405678

I Can Speak Bully

Written by Kevin Morrison

Illustrated by Mai S. Kemble

Ambassador
Children's Books
New York/Mahwah, NJ

REGENCY PARK
BRANCH

For Sean in first grade, Takashi in second, and Chet in Jr. High.
I'm a better friend now. —K.M.

For Ethan Sean, Eva Marie, Maya Rose, Graden, Bryce, & Keegan Daichi.
Be strong, happy, and make many friends. —M.S.K.

Text copyright © 2009 by Kevin Morrison
Illustrations copyright © 2009 by Mai S. Kemble

All rights reserved. No part of this book may be reproduced or transmitted in any form or by any means, electronic or mechanical, including photocopying, recording, or by any information storage and retrieval system without permission in writing from the Publisher.

Library of Congress Cataloging-in-Publication Data

Morrison, Kevin, 1973-
  I can speak Bully / written by Kevin Morrison ; illustrated by Mai S.
Kemble.
     p. cm.
  Summary: When a boy asks his mother how to deal with the school bully,
she tells him to speak the other boy's language and try to be his
friend.
  ISBN 978-0-8091-6744-9 (alk. paper)
  [1. Stories in rhyme. 2. Bullies--Fiction. 3. Friendship--Fiction.] I.
Kemble, Mai S., ill. II. Title.
  PZ8.3.M826Iac 2009
  [E]--dc22
                          2009004513

Published by Ambassador Books
An imprint of Paulist Press
997 Macarthur Boulevard
Mahwah, NJ 07430

www.ambassadorbooks.com

Printed and bound in China.

Where there is no love, put love—
and you will find love.

— St. John of the Cross

The world is full of many wonderful people and many wonderful languages.

Some people speak English.
Some speak Chinese.
Some people speak Spanish.
Some speak Portuguese.
Some people speak loudly.
Some speak softly.
Then there is me.
I can speak Bully.

But I had to learn.

There once was a boy in my
class who was a Bully;

an awfully mean,
awfully bad,
awfully big,
and awfully mad Bully.

His seat was next to mine,
and I dreaded going to school.
I didn't want to see the Bully
and be treated like a fool.

He scribbled on my homework.

He grabbed my lunch dessert.

He punched my arms
and kicked my legs
and even ripped my shirt.

He told me I'm too short.
He said that I'm too fat.

He told me I'm a loser,

and I really don't like that.

I cried, "Oh Mother, Mother!
What am I to do?
I ignored him like you said I should!
Now my limbs are black and blue."

Mother smiled a gentle smile
and patted me on the head.
She didn't talk for quite a while;
then this is what she said:

"Perhaps the boy is really sad because he's had it rough.
It may be that he's not so bad and that he's acting tough."

"Maybe if he had a friend, he wouldn't be so blue.
Maybe if YOU were his friend, he'd be a friend to you."

"Oh, Mother you are very wrong! It's not friendship that he's after!
He's big and mean and very strong and pain brings on his laughter!

"He doesn't want to talk to me.
He only wants to hit!
Instead of words, he speaks in
Bully, and I don't understand it!"

Mother smiled with a gleam in her eye.
"Maybe you do.

"I bet he wants to make some friends.
And I bet that you do, too.
I bet he wants to have some fun,
and he's a lot like you.

"You know this Bully
better than you think you do.
Be nice to him.
And I bet he'll be nice to you."

With love and care and wisdom, too, my mother taught me what to do.
"Start with a smile and a 'How are you, today?'
He won't know what hit him. He won't know what to say.

But do it again. Don't hesitate. Perseverance,"
Mom said, "will make a good person great."

So I did it.

I sat down with a smile
and gave him a "Hello."
He looked at me strangely,
and I thought he might blow.

He scribbled on my homework for old time's sake.

He tried to sound mean, but it seemed a little fake.

So I did it again.

I gave him a treat
from my brown lunch bag,
and I cringed in my seat
in case he got mad.
He opened his mouth
unsure of what to say,

but finally he spoke,
"What's with you today?"

"Nothing," I said
grinning, ear to ear.
"I just want you to know
I'm glad you're here.
If you want to be friends,
I wouldn't mind.
I know that sometimes
friends are hard to find."

He sat up straight and
puffed out his chest,
"I don't need friends
like all the rest!"

But then he slouched down

and looked a little sad,

"But if you'd be my friend,
I sure would be glad."

I'm sure Mom was smiling
with a gleam in her eye.
She was right.
It worked.
I just had to try.

I learned to speak Bully
and now I understand,
but the best part is:

now my Bully speaks Friend.